W9-CGM-182

PROFESSOR COOK'S MIND-BLOWING BAKING

Enslow Publishers, Inc.
40 Industrial Road
Box 398
Berkeley Heights, NJ 07922
USA
http://www.enslow.com

This edition published by Enslow Publishers Inc.

All rights reserved.

No part of this book may be reproduced by any means without the written permission of the publisher.

Library of Congress Cataloging-in-Publication Data:

Brash, Lorna.
  Professor Cook's Mind-Blowing Baking/ Lorna Brash.
    pages cm. — (Professor Cook's ...)
  Audience: 9-12
  Audience: Grade 4 to Grade 6
  Summary: "Over a dozen different dinner recipes and each recipe has a short science bit explaining the mysteries of food" —Provided by publisher.
  Includes bibliographical references.
  ISBN 978-0-7660-4303-9
  1. Baking— Juvenile literature. I. Title II. Series
  TX 773.S3547 2013
  641.8'15—-dc23

2012031115

Future edition:
  Paperback ISBN: 978-1-4644-0551-8

To Our Readers:
We have done our best to make sure all Internet addresses in this book were active and appropriate when we went to press. However, the auth and the publisher have no control over and assume no liability for the material available on those Internet sites or on other Web sites they may link to. Any comments or suggestions can be sent by e-mail to comments@enslow.com or to the address on the back cover.

Printed in China

012013 WKT, Shenzhen, Guangdong, China

10 9 8 7 6 5 4 3 2 1

First published in the UK in 2012 by Wayland

Copyright © Wayland 2012

Wayland
 338 Euston Rd
 London NW1 3BH

Editor: Debbie Foy
Designer: Lisa Peacock
Photographer: Ian Garlick
Proofreader/indexer: Sarah Doughty
Consultant: Sean Connolly

Wayland is a division of Hachette Children's Boo
an Hachette UK company.
www.hachette.co.uk

CONTENTS

PROFESSOR COOK'S... INCREDIBLE EDIBLES

Are you hungry to learn more about your food?

Have you ever wondered why some foods behave the way they do? For example, have you ever wondered how simply delicious meringue is made from little old egg whites? Or how ice cream can be baked (yes, baked!) in a hot oven without it melting—not even a little bit? Find out the answers to these questions and more with Professor Cook and the team!

Discover how to make hot ice cream sparkle, cupcakes with an explosive twist, and delicious bread baked in a seedy flowerpot! Approach the black & blue buns with caution (only because they are so dangerously nutritious)! Oh, and don't have nightmares over our super-cheesy oozing crust pizza!

Happy ~~Experimenting~~ Cookin

PROFESSOR COOK'S KITCHEN RULE BOOK

→ Wash your hands before you start cooking and after handling raw stuff, like meat

→ Mop up spills as soon as they happen

→ Use oven gloves for handling hot dishes straight from the oven

→ Listen up! Take care with sharp knives. Don't walk around with them!

→ Turn off the oven or stovetop when you have finished cooking

→ Use separate cutting boards for vegetables and meat

→ Raw and cooked foods should be kept separate in the fridge

→ Don't forget to tidy up the kitchen afterwards! No-brainer, huh?

ABBREVIATIONS

c = cup

tsp = teaspoon

tbsp = tablespoon

oz = ounce

°F = degree Fahrenheit

HOT GOODS!

WHEN YOU SEE THIS WARNING SIGN AN ADULT'S HELP MAY BE NEEDED!

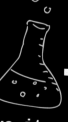

The "Science Bits"

Believe it or not, cooking involves a lot of science!
The Science Bits that accompany each of Professor Cook's delicious recipes answer all the mysteries about food that you have ever wanted to know.
They also explore some of the interesting, unusual, or quirky ways that our food often behaves!

Stuff you need:

1/2 c unsalted butter

1/2 c light brown sugar

1 medium egg

1 1/2 tsp vanilla extract

1/2 tsp baking powder

1 2/5 c plain flour

1 1/2 oz buttermilk

1 tbsp red cochineal food coloring (or red food coloring)

1/3 c cream cheese

1 c confectioner's sugar, plus extra for dusting

Makes 13 pies

HOT GOODS!

These bright red little treats are made with a natural red food coloring and buttermilk — a secret ingredient that makes your cakes deliciously soft — just like velvet!

Step 1

Preheat the oven to 350°F. Line two baking sheets with parchment paper. Trace a 2-in plain cookie cutter to mark out 26 light pencil circles on the parchment paper. Turn the paper over.

CRIMSON VELVET WHOOPIE PIES!

Step 2

Beat together 1/3 c butter and all the brown sugar until pale and fluffy. Add the egg and 1 tsp vanilla extract. Beat again until smooth. Add the baking powder, flour, buttermilk, and coloring. Whisk for 1 minute only, until well combined.

Step 3

Drop teaspoonfuls of the cake mixture onto the traced circles and spread until it just fills them. Bake for 12–15 minutes. After 10 minutes cooling, transfer to a wire rack to cool completely.

Step 4

Beat the remaining butter with the cream cheese, remaining vanilla extract, and confectioner's sugar. Sandwich the red cakes together with the creamy filling. Dust with confectioner's sugar. Delicious!

The Science Bit

Is cochineal really made from beetles?

Well, yes and no. The stuff we call cochineal is a chemical extract of carminic acid made from the bodies of crushed female scale insects from South and Central America! But they are not beetles. Don't let this put you off cochineal though. This red pigment has been used for centuries by the Aztecs and American Indians!

CHOCCY CHOUX PUFFS

Stuff you need:

1/3 c unsalted butter
1/2 c strong plain flour
2 large eggs, beaten
1 1/4 c double cream
1 tbsp confectioner's sugar
1/3 c dark chocolate
1/3 c white chocolate

Makes 8

HOT GOODS!

Choux is pronounced like "shoe" but is as light and fluffy as a cloud! So how are these so scrumptiously yummy AND so perfectly puffy?

Step 1

Preheat the oven to 400°F. Place 1/4 c of butter into a pan and add 5 oz water. Heat until the butter melts, then turn up the heat until the water boils. Remove the pan from the heat and add all the flour. Beat with a wooden spoon until the mixture forms a soft ball in the center of the pan. Allow to cool.

Step 2

Whisk the beaten eggs, a spoonful at a time, into the cooled mixture until smooth. Place evenly spaced spoonfuls of mixture onto two wet baking sheets. Bake for 10 minutes, then increase the oven temperature to 425°F. Bake for a further 15 minutes. Remove from the oven and transfer to a wire rack. Make a slit in the sides of the buns to allow the steam to escape.

Step 3

Whip the cream until thick and stir in the confectioner's sugar. Spoon into the split buns.

Step 4

Roughly chop the white and dark chocolate. Melt each in separate bowls over a pan of hot water, with half of the remaining butter added to each bowl. Allow to cool for 10 minutes before dipping the buns in the melted chocolate. Sprinkle with flaked chocolate to decorate!

The Science Bit

What makes choux pastry so puffy?

Choux has a high water content and when it is baked in the oven, the water evaporates to form steam. But that steam cannot escape because the protein in the eggs binds the outside of the dough "balloon" so that it remains puffy once you have let the air escape from the slit!

EXPLODING CUPCAKES!

Popping candy is a cracking good topping to sprinkle on your cupcakes! But where does popping candy get its big bang?

Stuff you need:

For the cupcakes:
2/3 c unsalted butter
2/3 c superfine sugar
1 2/5 c self-rising flour
3 medium eggs
1 tsp vanilla extract

For the frosting:
1 1/3 c unsalted butter
2 1/4 confectioner's sugar
1 1/2 tsp vanilla extract
Food colorings

To decorate:
Popping candy
Edible glitter sprinkles

Makes 18 cupcakes

HOT GOODS!

Step 1

Preheat the oven to 350°F. Line two muffin tins with baking cups. Place all the cupcake ingredients into a bowl and whisk for 2 minutes.

Step 2

Divide the mixture evenly between the cups. Bake for 18–20 minutes until golden. Transfer to a wire rack to cool.

Step 3

For the frosting, beat the butter and confectioner's sugar until smooth. Add the vanilla and 2–3 tbsp hot water and beat again. Divide the mixture into bowls and add a few drops of food coloring to each bowl.

Step 4

Use a piping bag to add swirls of frosting on to your cupcakes. Sprinkle with popping candy and edible glitter. Eat right away for cakes that are sure to be a blast!

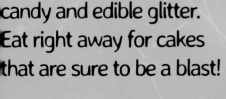

The Science Bit

What gives popping candy its big bang?

Popping candy is made like other hard candy, except that carbon dioxide (CO_2) is added at high pressure when the mixture of sugar, lactose, corn syrup, and flavorings have been heated to boiling point. The CO_2 stays "trapped" in bubbles, with walls that harden as the candy cools. When the candy hits your tongue and melts, the high-pressure CO_2 escapes with a loud "pop"!

Stuff you need:

16 oz puff pastry, thawed if frozen
2 tbsp plain flour, for dusting
14 oz can custard
1 tsp vanilla extract
Grated rind of 1 lemon
2 medium eggs
2 tbsp confectioner's sugar

Makes 10 tarts

HOT GOODS!

An egg is a giant single cell, just like the cells that make up your body!

The Science Bit

How does custard change from a liquid to a solid?

The process of changing a liquid protein (the custard) to a solid (the set custard filling) is called coagulation, and this is done by heating. Custard is a mixture of eggs, milk, and sugar. When heated, the protein in the eggs and milk coagulates to change the texture of the food.

SQUIDGY WIDGY CUSTARD TARTS

Crisp on the outside and squidgy on the inside — these custard tarts are irresistible. One will not be enough!

Step 1

Preheat the oven to 375°F. Roll out the pastry on a floured surface to about 1/2 in thick and 12 x 16–in (in area.) Cut out 10 circles of about 4–in (in diameter). Use them to line a muffin tin.

Step 2

Whisk together the custard, vanilla, lemon rind, and eggs and pour into the pastry cases. Bake for 35–40 minutes until the filling is set. Allow to cool completely before transferring them to a baking tray.

Step 3

Dust the tarts thickly with confectioner's sugar and grill under a high heat for 2 minutes or until the sugar starts to brown and caramelize.

OOZING CRUST PIZZA

This pizza features stretchy mozzarella cheese as a topping but also as a filling for the pizza crust. Cheese-o-rama!

Stuff you need:

5 oz pizza dough mix
1 tbsp flour, for dusting
1 ball mozzarella cheese, diced
2 tbsp sun-dried tomato paste
4 cherry plum tomatoes, halved
Handful fresh basil leaves

Serves 2

HOT GOODS!

Step 1

Preheat the oven to 425°F. Make the pizza dough mix according to the instructions. Knead the dough on a lightly floured surface until smooth and elastic. Press out into a 10-in circle.

Step 2

Arrange half the mozzarella around the dough edge in a circle about 1/2 in from the edge. Wet the edge of the dough and gently lift it over the cheese. Press down to enclose it all the way around. Allow the dough to rise in a warm place for 15 minutes.

Step 3

Spread the tomato paste over the pizza base and add the remaining mozzarella, cherry tomatoes, and basil leaves over the top. Bake for 12–15 minutes until the cheese has melted.

As you heat mozzarella the proteins uncoil and become stringy and elastic!

The Science Bit

Cheese gives you nightmares: science fact or urban myth?

If you go to bed with a full stomach, you may spend more of the night in REM (rapid eye movement) sleep, which is when your most vivid dreams occur. But there is no evidence to suggest that cheese causes your dreams to be bad.
Conclusion: URBAN MYTH!

VERY BERRY CHOCO RIPPLE MERINGUE

These snowy peaks of magic are made from a combination of everyday ingredients. Crisp on the outside and chewy on the inside, the texture is simply irresistible!

Stuff you need:

3 egg whites
3/4 c superfine sugar
2 tbsp cocoa powder
1 1/3 c whipped cream
Mixed fresh berries

Makes 6

Step 1

Preheat the oven to 250°F. Whisk the egg whites with an electric hand whisk until just stiff. You should be able to hold the bowl over your head without any falling out! While whisking, add the sugar a spoonful at a time until the meringue becomes thick and glossy.

Step 2

Sift the cocoa powder over the meringue and fold in with a metal spoon to achieve a "rippled" effect.

Step 3

Line a baking sheet with parchment paper and spoon on 6 piles of meringue. Bake for 2 hours. Turn the oven off and leave the meringues in the oven for a further hour. Serve piled with whipped cream and fresh berries!

The crispness of meringue depends on how much sugar is beaten into the egg whites!

The Science Bit

Can meringues ever change back into egg whites?

No. When we whisk egg whites we are breaking down the protein chains in the structure of the egg white. This process is called "denaturing." As the denaturing of protein cannot be reversed, this process is known as an irreversible change. So, meringues, listen up! You will never be egg whites again!

KITCHEN SINK POTPIES

Everything-but-the-kitchen-sink can be thrown in to these yummy potpies to really get your taste buds a-jangling!

Stuff you need:

2 3/4 c plain flour
3/4 c unsalted butter, diced
6 oz rindless bacon, chopped
2 chicken breasts, finely diced
Handful fresh thyme, chopped
3 1/2 oz Cheddar cheese, diced
6 tbsp applesauce
1 medium egg, beaten
1 tsp salt
Freshly ground black pepper

Makes 9 pies

HOT GOODS!

Step 1

Whiz the flour and butter in a food processor until the mixture resembles fine breadcrumbs. Add 4–5 tbsp water until the mixture forms a pastry. Allow to chill for 30 minutes.

Step 2

Preheat the oven to 400°F. Roll out two-thirds of the pastry and use a 4-in cutter to stamp out 9 circles to line a muffin tin.

Step 3

Fry the bacon, chicken, and thyme over a medium heat for 7–8 minutes, stirring occasionally until cooked through. Stir in the cheese and applesauce. Spoon the mixture into pastry cases.

The Science Bit

What is "umami"?

Umami is one of the 5 flavors (including salt, sweet, sour, and bitter) that human beings can detect through receptor cells on their tongues. The word "umami" was first used by a Japanese professor who discovered that various foods contained this savory, meaty flavor. Foods with a high umami content are red meats, fish such as anchovies, sardines, and tuna, seafood, soy sauce, tomatoes, and cheese.

Step 4

Roll out the remaining pastry and stamp out 3 1/2 x 3–in circles. Wet the edges of the circles and press them down firmly onto the filled pastry cases. Brush the pie tops with beaten egg and season with salt and pepper. Bake for 25–30 minutes until golden. Allow to cool in the tin for 10–15 minutes before tucking in!

HOT ICE CREAM SPARKLE

Stuff you need:

2 chocolate muffins
2 c ice cream
4 medium eggs
1 c superfine sugar
Edible glitter sprinkles

Serves 4

HOT GOODS!

How can you bake ice cream in a hot oven without it melting? Make this amazing hot-but-cold dessert, then serve it to your friends!

The Science Bit

How can you bake ice cream without it melting?

When we whisk up meringue we make loads of little pockets of air in the mixture! When the meringue is spooned over the ice cream all those nifty air pockets act as insulators that prevent warm air from getting inside and melting the ice cream! The heat from the oven also starts to caramelize the sugar in the meringue and forms a delicious golden brown crust on the outside, which forms a protective layer over the

Step 1

Halve the muffins horizontally and place the 4 pieces equally spaced onto a baking sheet. Pile a quarter of the ice cream over each muffin and place in the freezer until ready to use. Preheat the oven to 450°F.

Step 2

Whisk the egg whites with an electric hand whisk until they are stiff and will stay in the bowl when it is upturned! While whisking, add the sugar a spoonful at a time. The meringue will become white, thick, and glossy.

Step 3

Cover the muffins and ice cream with the meringue, working quickly before the ice cream melts. Ensure you "fill in" any holes that will allow heat in to melt the ice cream. Bake immediately for 3–4 minutes until golden brown. Sprinkle with edible glitter and serve.

SUPER SEEDY FLOWERPOT BREAD

You don't even need to be a green-fingered gardener to watch these delicious mini flowerpot loaves grow. All you need to do is awaken the yeast!

Step 1

Preheat the oven to 425°F. Wash the pots in hot soapy water. Rinse and pat dry. Brush them inside and out with oil and place on a baking tray. Bake for 10 minutes. Very carefully remove from the oven and allow to cool completely. Turn off the oven.

Stuff you need:

- 6 small, new terra-cotta flowerpots
- 4 tbsp vegetable oil
- 1 tbsp softened butter
- 1/2 oz sesame seeds
- 1/2 oz poppy seeds
- 1 oz pumpkin seeds
- 1 oz sunflower seeds
- 1 tbsp dark corn syrup
- 1 package (1/4 oz) instant yeast
- 4 cups whole-wheat flour
- 2 tbsp milk

Makes 6 bread pots

HOT GOODS!

Step 2

Brush the insides of the pots with softened butter. Mix all the seeds together and sprinkle half onto the buttery insides. Tip upside down and save any seeds that do not stick.

Step 3

Mix the dark corn syrup with 1/2 c warm water. Stir in the yeast and allow to sit for 5 minutes to "foam." Sift the flour into a bowl and stir in the yeast mixture. Add 1 3/4 c warm water and half the remaining seeds. Use your hands to form a soft dough.

Step 4

Knead the dough for 3-4 minutes until smooth. Divide into 6 balls and place into the pots. Brush with milk and scatter over any remaining seeds. Leave the pots to rise in a warm place for 30 minutes until the dough doubles in size. Preheat the oven to 450°F. Bake the pots on a baking tray for 15 -20 minutes. Serve warm or cold.

The Science Bit

Is yeast really a living organism?

Yes it is! Yeast is actually lots of tiny microscopic fungi (mushroom relatives) that are activated by warmth, moisture, and sugar. When we leave dough to rise in a warm place, the yeast in the dough converts natural sugars from the flour into gases that are trapped in the bread. These gases are responsible for all the little holes you can see in a slice of bread, and which create pockets for your jam or peanut butter!

23

STACK 'EM HIGH CHEESY PUFF PIE

What turns a thick cheese sauce into a deliciously light and airy souffle when baked? Read on...

Stuff you need:

- 1/3 c unsalted butter
- 1/4 c fine fresh white breadcrumbs
- 1/3 c plain flour
- 1/2 tsp English mustard powder
- 1 oz whole milk
- 3 1/2 oz mature Cheddar cheese, grated
- 4 large eggs, separated

Serves 6

HOT GOODS!

Step 1

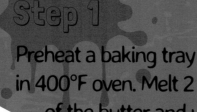

Preheat a baking tray in 400°F oven. Melt 2 tbsp of the butter and use it to brush the insides of six 8-oz ramekins. Sprinkle with the fine breadcrumbs to coat and set aside.

Step 2

Melt the remaining butter in a saucepan. Add the flour and mustard powder and stir for 1 minute over a low heat. Gradually add the milk and stir until the sauce thickens. Remove from the heat and stir in the cheese and egg yolks. Beat well.

Step 3

Use an electric hand whisk to beat the egg whites until stiff. Stir a large spoonful of whites into the cheese sauce to "loosen" the mixture. Using a metal spoon gently fold the remaining whites into the sauce. Spoon into the ramekins, filling just to the rim. Clean the ramekin rims with a paper towel to allow the souffle to rise evenly.

Step 4

Carefully remove the hot baking sheet from the oven and place the ramekins onto it. Bake the mini souffles for 8–10 minutes, until golden. Serve and eat immediately.

The Science Bit

What makes souffle so light and airy?

Air is the most important ingredient in a souffle and is the reason why it rises! When the egg whites are folded into the cheese sauce the fats in the sauce coat the air bubbles in the whites. When heat is applied, the air inside the egg whites expands and "inflates" it. But eat it quickly, because as soon as the air inside is lost the souffle will deflate!

Stuff you need:

1 tbsp butter, melted
3 medium eggs
1/3 c superfine sugar
1 c plain flour
1 tsp easy-blend yeast
1/4 c warm milk
3/4 c blueberries
1 c blackberries
2 tbsp confectioner's sugar

Makes 12

HOT GOODS!

Blueberries are full of antioxidants, which help to combat and eliminate toxins in our bodies

The Science Bit

Why are blueberries so super?

These little purple berries really are a powerhouse of good stuff! One of the top 10 superfoods ever, they are high in vitamin C, antioxidants, and fiber, all of which are excellent for keeping your skin in good condition as well as fighting diseases like cancer, heart disease, and asthma. Scientists also say that blueberries keep your brain more active. Pass the blueberries, please!

BLACK & BLUE BUNS

Don't be fooled by the name of these buns. They are totally and utterly good for you as they contain an amazingly talented superfood...

Step 1

Preheat the oven to 425°F. Brush a 12-hole muffin tin with melted butter.

Step 2

Whisk together the eggs, sugar, and flour until smooth. Mix the yeast and warm milk together until smooth and whisk into the egg mixture. Pour evenly into the prepared muffin tin.

Step 3

Scatter the blueberries and blackberries into the center of each bun. Bake for 12–15 minutes until golden brown. Dust with the confectioner's sugar to serve.

Stuff you need:

3/4 c unsalted butter
1 c superfine sugar
1 medium egg
1 tsp vanilla extract
3 1/4 plain flour, plus extra
   for dusting
32 plain hard candies

Makes 32 cookies

HOT GOODS!

Human beings are "programmed" through evolution to enjoy sweet foods!

Stained glass candy in a cookie, all rolled into one — it's magic!

Step 1

Preheat the oven to 350°F. Line two baking trays with parchment paper. Cream the butter and sugar until pale. Stir in the egg and vanilla extract. Fold in the flour, and add 1–2 tbsp water to form a dough. Wrap the dough in plastic wrap and chill for 30 minutes.

STAINED GLASS COOKIES

Step 2

Unwrap the dough and cut in half. On a floured surface, roll half of the dough to a 1/10 in thickness. Using 4-in cookie cutters cut shapes from the dough and place on the baking sheets. Repeat with the remaining dough.

Step 3

Use a 1-in cutter to stamp circles from the center of your cookies and put a hard candy into the hole. Bake for 10 minutes. Tilt the tray to allow the melted sweets to fill the holes. Cool for 5 minutes, then transfer to a wire rack to cool completely.

The Science Bit

Are hard candies <u>really</u> boiled?

Yes! A hard candy is a concentrated sugar solution. As sugar and water are heated, the water boils away and the sugar concentrates as the temperature of the mixture rises. The highest temperature and most concentrated sugar solution results in hard candies, which become hard and brittle (rather than chewy) when cooled.

PROFESSOR COOK'S GLOSSARY

ANTIOXIDANTS substances in our food that help to rid our bodies of toxins, slow down cell damage, and protect us from disease

BEAT a quick and vigorous mix with a spoon or whisk

BLEND to mix two or more ingredients together

BUTTERMILK the slightly sour liquid left over after butter has been churned

CARAMELIZE the process that happens to sugar when it is heated. It converts to caramel

CELL basic unit of all living things

COAGULATION when protein molecules or chains rearrange themselves, break, or change

EVOLUTION a process of development through which something changes into a different and more complex form

FIBER a substance found in some foods that adds bulk to our food and aids digestion

FRY to cook food with oil in a shallow frying pan

FUNGI the name given to a group of living things, which includes yeast for making bread

INSULATOR material or object that does not allow heat to easily pass through it

IRREVERSIBLE (CHANGES) describes something that cannot be changed back

KNEAD to fold, push, and pull dough with your hands until it becomes soft and smooth

MOLECULES the smallest units of a chemical substance or compound

PROTEIN the second most common substance in our body (after water),

elping us to grow and fight disease

...AMEKIN a miniature cooking dish
...ften used for souffles

...EM stands for Rapid Eye Movement.
... is a deep sleep state in which
...reams can occur

...ISE when a dough is left in a warm
...lace to rise

...CALE INSECT a type of small
...nsect that produces a waxy coating
...the "scale") as protection

...IEVE to strain a liquid or push
...omething through a sieve to get
...id of lumps

...OLUTION a liquid containing a dissolved
...olid or gas

SUPERFOODS
nutrient-rich foods
that can help to
fight off aging and
illness

TOXINS poisonous
substances produced
by cells

uMAMI a Japanese word meaning
"pleasant savory taste." It is one
of the five basic tastes

WHISK to mix
something quickly
to get air into it

YEAST an agent
used to raise
dough in bread
making

INDEX

USEFUL WEB SITES

www.spatulatta.com
Get some basic cooking skills under your belt, with step-by-step video recipes and a recipe box that includes options for cooking a meal by choosing a basic ingredient, a type of food, occasion, or particular diet.

www.yummyscience.co.uk
Super-fun science projects to try out in the kitchen using everyday foods. Grow your own crystals with salt, test out the toasting properties of bread, or make your own honeycomb toffee. Some of these recipes call for an adult's help, so always make sure you let an adult know before you start.

www.exploratorium.edu/cooking
Find out how a pinch of curiosity can improve your cooking! Explore recipes, activities, and webcasts that will improve your understanding of the science behind food and cooking.

Professor Cook's Dynamite Dinners

978-0-7660-4301-5

Professor Cook's Incredible Edibles!
Sticky Chicky Burger Stacks
Tex-Mex
Taco Bowl Salad
Incredible Edible Bowl Soup!
Posh Fish 'n' Chips 'n' Dip!
Boost Your Burger!
Finger Lickin' Chicken Satay
Japan-Easy Tuna Rolls
Tongue-Tingling Sweet and Sour Noodles
Thirsty Couscous Cakes!
Scrambly Egg Fried Rice
Superfood Cannelloni
Chili with a Deep, Dark Secret
Professor Cook's Glossary
Index & Useful Web Sites

Professor Cook's Mind-Blowing Baking

978-0-7660-4303-9

Professor Cook's Incredible Edibles!
Crimson velvet whoopie pies!
Choccy choux puffs
Exploding cupcakes!
Squidgy widgy custard tarts
Oozing crust pizza
Very berry choco ripple meringues
Kitchen sink potpies
Hot ice cream sparkle
Super seedy flowerpot bread
Stack 'em high cheesy puff pie
Black & blue buns
Stained glass cookies
Professor Cook's Glossary
Index & Useful Web Sites

Professor Cook's Fruity Desserts

978-0-7660-4302-2

Professor Cook's Incredible Edibles!
Tropical fruit with goo-ey chocolate dip
Incredible edible tie-dye ice pops
Icy watermelon fruit slices
Hot pineapple "lollies"
Super blueberry cheesecake
Wobbly strawberry mousse
"Magic" apple & blackberry pudding
Ice bowl fruit salad
Nicey slicey summer fruit jelly
Homemade yogurt with fruit squish
Instant frozen yogurt
Sticky licky banoffee cones
Professor Cook's Glossary
Index & Useful Web Sites

Professor Cook's Smashing Snacks

978-0-7660-4304-6

Professor Cook's Incredible Edibles!
Pop-tastic popcorn
Smashing caramel shards
Ice cream in a bag
Cheese-and-ham-o-rama!
Homemade beans on toast
Oat-so yummy power cookies
"No-cry" onion bhajis & dip
Double-dipped mallow cookies
Mini superhero pies!
Gold bullion honeycomb bars!
Pink fizzbomb lemonade
Big dipper breadsticks
Professor Cook's Glossary
Index & Useful Web Sites